CONSCIOUS
Living

BK Ritu Thakkar

BLUEROSE PUBLISHERS
India | U.K.

Copyright © Ritu Girish Thakkar 2024

All rights reserved by author. No part of this publication may be reproduced, stored in a retrieval system or transmitted in any form or by any means, electronic, mechanical, photocopying, recording or otherwise, without the prior permission of the author. Although every precaution has been taken to verify the accuracy of the information contained herein, the publisher assumes no responsibility for any errors or omissions. No liability is assumed for damages that may result from the use of information contained within.

BlueRose Publishers takes no responsibility for any damages, losses, or liabilities that may arise from the use or misuse of the information, products, or services provided in this publication.

For permissions requests or inquiries regarding this publication, please contact:

BLUEROSE PUBLISHERS
www.BlueRoseONE.com
info@bluerosepublishers.com
+91 8882 898 898
+4407342408967

ISBN: 978-93-5989-197-2

Cover design: Siddharth Shete Patil
Typesetting: Namrata Saini

First Edition: April 2024

Preface

Remember a day in your life, when you were completely content and happy with every aspect of your life – self, family, friends, career, health. Are you able to recollect one particular day of your life like this? Or is it a bit difficult?

Happiness is a basic human emotion that every human being is seeking or looking for. And yet people find it difficult to find even a day when there is a constant feeling of happiness throughout the day.

The reason why you are looking so hard, but not able to find happiness is because, in today's world, we are made to believe happiness is out there, in things, relationships, or achievements. However, this book aims at decoding happiness and simplifying its experience in our everyday life.

Conscious living is an aware way of living beyond the unconscious thinking pattern of the mind. It is about living the little joys of life in every moment and not postponing happiness for a future date.

Acknowledgment

This book is a culmination of all the learnings that I have had through various situations of life. Every situation that I have faced and handled in my life journey, has given me deeper insights into the functioning of spiritual laws. They have also taught me ways of managing my thoughts and emotions through every scene and taking charge of my happiness irrespective of outside situations. I am extremely grateful to life for giving me an opportunity to learn and grow and thus being able to write this book as a result of these learnings.

In the journey of life, the Supreme has not just guided my every footstep but also walked me through it. This book would have never been possible without the inspiration and guidance from the Supreme. My heartfelt gratitude to the Supreme for all the blessings I have been bestowed upon.

My family has been my biggest support system to fall back on, in times of failure and success. I am extremely thankful to my family for always being by my side. I am and will be indebted to my family for all that I have received from them.

Lastly, I would like to thank each and every person who has directly or indirectly contributed to the making of this book.

Contents

Preface iii
Acknowledgment v
Contents vii
1. The Search for Happiness 1
2. The (Over) Thinking Mind 11
3. Living in the Stories of the Mind 22
4. Pain and Suffering 31
5. Ways to deal with Stories of the Mind 42
6. Relationship Healing 54
7. Ego Identification 66
8. The Being – and its Nature 80
9. Awakening to a Conscious Way of Living 90
10. The Higher Consciousness 100
11. Surrender – the Ultimate Human Experience 109

1. The Search for Happiness

Reflection Exercise:

1. Complete the following sentence:

    I will be happy when:

    1. _____
    2. _____
    3. _____

2. What does Happiness mean to you?

    _____

    _____

3. Where do you get Happiness from?

    _____

    _____

4. Who / What is responsible for UnHappiness in your Life?

    _____

    _____

5. Do you want to "be happy in life" or do you want to "be happy sometimes in life"?

    _____

    _____

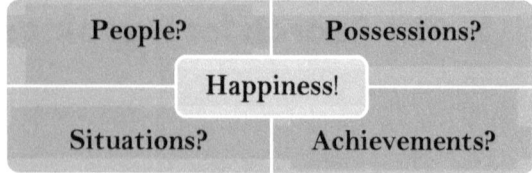

Have you ever encountered any of the below scenarios?

- Dressed well?
  But they did not like your attire.
- Made a good presentation?
  But they were able to find faults.
- Planned for a holiday?

But last-minute work requirements made you postpone your long-planned holiday.

- Worked hard for a business proposal?

  The client rejected the proposal saying it was not up to the mark.

What is your state of mind when the reality turns out to be different from your expectations, like in the above scenarios?

Source of Happiness or Unhappiness?

Everything that you thought was a source of your happiness (in the above scenarios – dress, presentation, holiday, or successful client closure), ended up becoming a source of your unhappiness. Have you ever had such an experience in life?

There are also times when you are working very hard to achieve some personal or professional goal of life. You are so focused on the achievement of the goal and postpone your happiness by saying "I will be happy when..". Just think about the moments, hours, weeks, and months you wait for happiness when you tie your happiness to Life Goals or situations. You may have also experienced this – by the time you achieve your goal, the next goal is ready even before you can fully experience happiness by achieving the earlier one.

This goes on like a spiral and most of the people end up living their lives postponing their happiness to some future date.

Looking for happiness in people, possessions, situations, and achievements is like looking for the lost key outside the house.

If the key is lost inside the house, that's where you will find it. Just because there is more light out there, you can't find it there anyway.

Happiness is a result of the way we think. Yet we keep looking for it outside as it is easier for most people to look there. Since our childhood, we haven't been taught to look inside to find happiness, but actually, that's where happiness lies.

It is because of looking at the wrong place, we do get momentary experiences of happiness, but they do not last long. Happiness thus becomes something that needs to be achieved or attained through doing instead of being. When we seek our happiness in people or situations, our happiness becomes conditional.

Happiness is an inside job and has very little or no connection with the external realities of life. You may have seen people who may get disturbed by slight aches or pains in the body whereas there are also people who manage to smile despite going through some terminal illness. External realities may or may not be our way. But the way we think and feel in every situation is a choice that we have. To be able to use this power of choice (to think and feel) is by putting it into use. It is like a machine, which when not used, becomes rusted.

Reference Point for Happiness

Ask yourself, how do you predict your happiness? What is the basis of making any decision for happiness?

Buying a good car will make me happy? Having my own house will make me happy? Being in a relationship or getting married will make me happy?

These are all predictions we make about happiness in the future.

A new car could make us unhappy instead of happy if someone makes a negative comment about the colour of the car.

Your own house could make you unhappy if your relations with people living inside are not good.

If all marriages resulted in happiness, then there would never have been divorces.

This helps us understand that we may or may not be good predictors of our happiness.

There are also many times when our reference point for finding happiness is the past. For example: I was happy in a certain job, city, or country and so I predict my happiness based on the past experience.

But this may not always be true. Sometimes what you consider your source of happiness based on the past, may not become your source of happiness in the future. A lot of researches prove otherwise that with a certain external stimulus using which you created happiness in the past, the repeat experience of happiness through the same stimulus will reduce the next time and will keep on reducing with every additional experience. For example, the pleasure that you experience with the first scoop of ice cream will be much higher than the pleasure you experience with the fifth scoop.

The reference point for happiness is neither in the past nor in the future. It is about living every moment with happiness in the present moment.

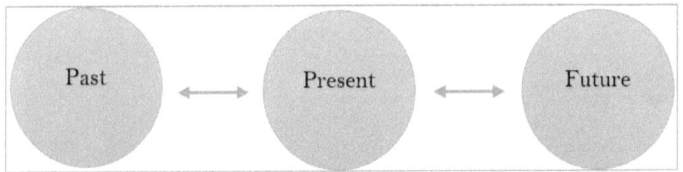

If you make happiness a destination that you have to strive to reach, you will keep striving one after the other, in a never-ending race. Instead, make happiness a journey where you cherish every bit that life is offering you in this moment.

Instead of doing things for happiness, do everything with happiness.

This requires a shift in our approach towards happiness.

Today, most people follow the "DO-GET-BE" approach towards happiness.

DO	Doing everything at an external level to achive goals, comforts and success
GET	Achive goals, comforts and success at an external level
BE	Be happy once you have achieved every at an external level

However, our search for happiness ceases to exist when we reverse the approach towards happiness as "BE-DO-GET".

BE	• Be happy. Know that happiness is a state of mind and an inside job.
DO	• Do everything with Happiness
GET	• When you do everything with happiness, you are able to do your best and achieve more.

With this new approach towards Happiness, happiness is not a once-in-a-while guest experience but a permanent resident in the house of your mind.

Constant and Consistent Happiness

Ask yourself - Do you want to "be happy in life" or do you want to "be happy sometimes in life"? What will be your response to this question?

Most people respond by saying that they want a happy life and not some moments of happiness in between life. And so it is important to understand that constant and consistent happiness cannot be found in externalities of life, and all external dimensions of life are variable. People may change, situations may turn out to be different from what we expect, and we may lose things we tag as ours. Depending your happiness on aspects that are variable, will give you conditional happiness but if you really want to experience constant and consistent happiness – you need to look at the source which is constant and consistent to you.

The one and only source that is constant and consistent to you is YOU - yourself. What does it mean – simply put, your thoughts and feelings are the only aspects that you can work upon and channelise. Happiness is a feeling that you experience and it is a result of thoughts that you create.

Two people living in the same house, going through similar life situations may have different experiences based on how they feel (stress or calmness, worry or care, hurt or forgiveness) depending on what they choose to think in that particular situation.

This also helps us get clarity that everything you thought was the source of your happiness, was not. For example – if the

Sun is the source of Heat and Light – it gives heat and light constantly and consistently. However, in the case of happiness, people or situations do not give us constant and consistent happiness.

This means there is an additional aspect that is responsible for creating our happiness or unhappiness. That additional aspect is - what you choose to think. The next question you may have is, do we really choose our thoughts? Well, you will get the answer to this in the upcoming chapters of this book.

Embracing Happiness

Coming back to Happiness – let me ask you a question – why is Happiness so important to you? Why do you seek Happiness in life?

To understand this, let us take an analogy of the body. Our body is made of 5 elements, the vital one being water. We seek water when we are thirsty, i.e. when the quantity of water reduces in the body.

Similarly, one of the elements of the Being (a Conscious Energy called Life or Life force) is Happiness. In the human journey, when the experience of happiness is reduced, we start seeking Happiness.

That is majorly the reason why most human beings are seeking happiness today. But not knowing where to look, spend their entire life just getting glimpses of what real joy or happiness could be.

Happiness is who we are – a happy being. The way to experience happiness is "being" in the consciousness of who we are – "a happy being". That is the way to access our innermost potent source of happiness. It is already there; we just need to look within through the eye of the mind to be able to see it (experience it).

It is just like light within, you just need to access it by switching it on. The switch is your mind – the thoughts that you create. Happiness is like an inner light that illuminates your inner world and the reflection of that inner light is seen in the world around you.

This simply means we give to others only what we have. When you have happiness stored within you, you share that feeling and vibrations with everyone you meet. The simplest way to share happiness is by being happy.

Every time you choose to create happy, peaceful, and loving thoughts – you access the inner treasures of these experiences.

Think-A-Thon

- ❖ I am responsible for my happiness.
- ❖ I choose to create happiness in every moment of my life, irrespective of outside situations.
- ❖ My potent source of happiness is within me.
- ❖ I am the constant and consistent source of happiness for myself.
- ❖ Happiness is the result of my own thoughts.
- ❖ I am happy in this moment and I radiate happy vibrations to everyone around.
- ❖ Happiness is who I am – a happy being.

2. The (Over) Thinking Mind

Reflection Exercise:

1. While you are reading this book, are you, alongside, thinking about something unknowingly?

   Are there any thoughts going on right now that you were not even aware of, before this reflection exercise?

   _____

2. Observe your thoughts – are these thoughts related to what you are reading or unrelated thoughts?

   _____

3. Are these thoughts anything about the past situation or future activity? Describe your thoughts a bit more.

   _____

   _____

   _____

4. Do you have similar thoughts quite often? If yes, how often?

   _____

   _____

The Unconscious Thinking Patterns

Have you observed that while actively being engaged in some activity, more often than not, the mind is unconsciously engaged in mental chattering which is unrelated to the act that you are actively involved in?

Even while you are reading this book right now, there may be some unrelated thoughts about a person or situation in the background of your mind. Like passing clouds, these thoughts may be passing by every moment.

If you observe deeply, most of these thoughts are repetitive, that is - you keep thinking about similar thoughts and experience the same kind of emotions repeatedly. This is called the thought pattern that you may have developed. Such a thought pattern makes us identified with certain thoughts and emotions. This is not a healthy state of mind as it is like compulsive thinking which may become a hindrance in your experience of life and activities that you do in everyday life.

It is very commonly experienced and heard these days that people forget if they have locked the door or switched off the light at home before leaving from home. Well, most of the time they have, but that action of doing it is not registered in the memory as there is unconscious thinking going on in the mind.

All these are signs of the mind which is absent from where the person is physically present. Important to note here, that most of these repetitive thoughts are also unnecessary, which means you do not put these thoughts into action. They are only like passing clouds which may not be of any practical use. These unconscious thinking patterns make these thoughts compulsive and drain a lot of mental energy due to constant mental noise.

Most of us have lived long enough with these unconscious thinking patterns that we do not even know if there is a way out of these patterns.

There is! We will discuss ways in which you can live life beyond these unconscious thinking patterns and experience life in its totality.

Mind's way to avoid Conscious Living

How many times has it happened to you that while your family member is talking to you, your mind is busy thinking about what happened at work? Suddenly in the middle of the conversation, you realise that you did not hear most of the part of the conversation.

If I ask you, were you present while that conversation was going on? You would say 'yes'. If yes, then who missed out most of the conversation?

While your body was present in that place, YOU were not, as your mind had taken you away from that place.

Let's understand why this happens. Imagine your mind as a big stage and your thoughts as actors. While there are some actors on the stage playing their roles, there

are some actors at the backstage waiting to play their part too. Actors on the stage are like the conscious thoughts on the stage of your mind – related to the action that you are performing at that time. Actors at the backstage are unconscious thoughts, which are mostly related to the past situations or the imagination of the future.

This is Mind's way to avoid conscious living by taking your attention away from the present moment. People who live in the past, mostly live in sadness, as most people recollect the past hurt more than their happy times. People who live in the future, experience anxiety and fear as the future is unknown.

I do understand that learning from the past is important. But what most people end up doing is replaying the past situation in their mind and experience the same emotions again in the mind to make the hurt even deeper instead of letting go of the hurt. This is not learning from the past.

Let's understand what learning from the past means:

- ✓ Look at the past situation from the third person's perspective.
- ✓ Do not get engaged with emotions in that situation.
- ✓ Do not judge the situation or people involved.
- ✓ Most Important: **Ask yourself, if a similar situation comes again in my life, what would I do differently and how would I respond differently?**

This is Learning from the past but not living in the past

Another important question to answer here is what is the difference between planning for the future and living in the future.

> **Let's understand what is difference between planning for the future and living in the future**
> - ✓ Planning for the future is focusing on what we need to do in terms of our actions.
>
>   Once planning is done, our energy goes into executing the plan.
>
> - ✓ Living in the future means making assumptions about the future situation and creating emotions basis the assumption, which have no real evidence of existence.

It is important to understand here that lessons from the past situation or event are relevant when they are applied now. Planning for the future is relevant when we work toward achieving a particular goal in the now.

Learning from the past is as important as planning for the future. But living in the emotions of the past and future can be quite harmful to the health of the mind. As the past and future are not a reality at the moment, there is nothing that can be done about the same. When you live in the past or future, then chances are that you feel powerless. Is there a way out of these experiences of emotions from the past and future? Sure, there is!

The mind is used to deny the awareness of the present moment and resist what is the current reality. However slow and steady practice to bring your attention to the present moment, whenever the past or future are not needed. Practice this in everyday life and slowly increase the practice.

Let's try the below step to initiate your inner journey towards the present.

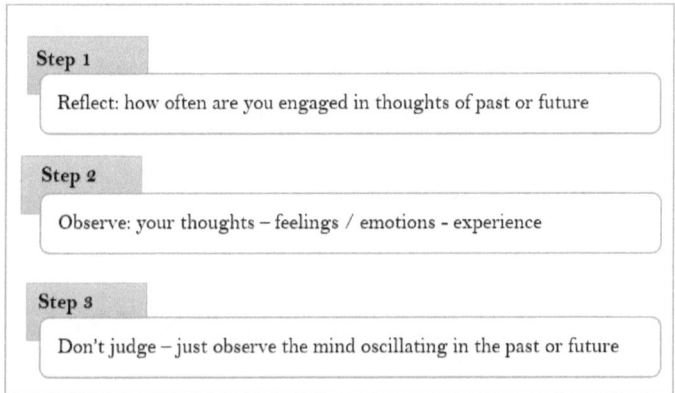

The doorway to overcoming the thoughts of the past and future is by creating an awareness of each moment, moment-by-moment; where life is happening. Life is neither happening in the past nor in the future – Life is happening in every second that is passing by and the same moment is becoming the past once that second has gone.

Let us try one simple exercise to experience living life where it is happening. You can do this exercise while doing your everyday routine work – like walking, cleaning, drinking water, eating food, or any other everyday activity.

Exercise: Live Life where it is happening

Example 1: While Walking

Step 1
As you start walking, bring your attention to yourself

Step 2
Pay attention to every step as you increase the speed

Step 3
Give your full attention to every movement of your body

Step 4
Observe any sound that may be coming from your steps

Step 5
Observe your breath as you walk

Exercise: Live Life where it is Happening

Example 2: While Drinking Water

Step 1
Become aware of glass that you are holding in your hand

Step 2
Be aware while you have the 1st sip of water

Step 3
Observe the effect and feel of water in your mouth

Step 4
Repeat it with every sip of water

Start with practicing the exercise on "Live Life where it is Happening" in small little ways in your everyday life. You will see how peace is growing in your life and how relaxed and at ease you start feeling.

This is also because neither the past nor the future is in our control. The past is no longer a reality for you to be able to change now. The future is not a reality anyway. Past and future are not reality but are only in our minds. And so we can't work on it or change it. We have no control over the past or the future.

Once you practice bringing your attention to the present moment in routine mundane activities, you will be able to experience the benefits of doing so in your everyday life. Slowly you can increase the practice while doing important activities like writing an email, preparing meals, etc., and then increase the practice by applying it to complex life situations. Deep awareness of the present moment is required in complex situations that trigger strong emotional reactions.

Another aspect related to the future is impatience while waiting for the end result. People experience impatience while waiting for little things in life like waiting for a response from a loved one or waiting at the red signal. Or it could be waiting for larger things in life like a better job or a bigger house. Well, let's understand why we feel impatient while waiting – it is because we want the future now. We ignore what we currently have and focus on what is possibly coming in the future. To overcome this habitual impatience is by acknowledging what you have in the present moment. Also, disassociate waiting at an external level to psychological waiting. You may wait for a message to come on your mobile, but not wait psychologically to feel impatient. You just bring your attention to what you currently have and work towards things that you are waiting for.

The only moment that is real is this moment. This is the moment that you can work on. This is the only moment where you can choose your thoughts, words, and actions and thus have control over it. Thinking about the past and future makes us feel powerless. Focusing on the present moment brings back our control to ourselves where we can use our power to choose.

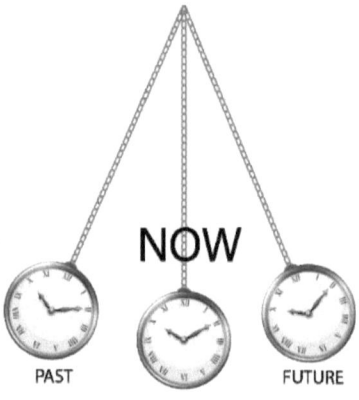

The more aware you are, the more peaceful you will feel. This is because you are no longer identified with your unconscious thinking pattern of the past or the future. You are more aware; you are more alive!

Practice focusing majorly on the present moment and everything that needs attention at this time.

Earlier you lived in the past and future, and only visited the present moment a few times a day. Reverse this equation: Live in the moment and visit the past and future for the practical purpose of learning from the past and planning for the future only.

Think-A-Thon

- ❖ To learn from the past, ask yourself, if a similar situation comes again in my life, what would you do differently and how would you respond differently?
- ❖ Planning for the future is focusing on what we need to do in terms of our actions.
- ❖ Once planning is done, our energy goes into executing the plan.
- ❖ We must learn from the past and plan for the future but don't live life there.
- ❖ Past and future are only in our mind, present moment is our reality.
- ❖ Living life where it is happening makes us feel peaceful and at ease.
- ❖ This is the only moment where you can choose your thoughts, words, and actions and thus have control over it.
- ❖ Living in the moment makes us more aware and alive!

3. Living in the Stories of the Mind

Reflection Exercise:

Sit by yourself for 10 minutes, without using any gadgets or doing any activity. No one and nothing to accompany you for 10 minutes. Observe yourself throughout this exercise.

1. Were you able to sit by yourself (without anyone or anything) for 10 minutes?

   _____

2. Was there an urge to use any gadget or access your social media in those 10 minutes?

   _____

3. Did your mind wander in the stories of the past or the future?

   _____

4. What were your thoughts and emotions during those 10 minutes?

   _____
   _____

5. Were you feeling comfortable and could sit for longer, if asked to? Or was there a sense of discomfort and you were waiting for 10 minutes to get over?

   _____
   _____

Unattended Mental Noise

Have you ever wondered why there is constant noise on the screen of our mind? Most of the time this noise is related to some past hurt or some future happening that we are not sure about. There is a reason why most people find it difficult to spend time by themselves and so keep themselves busy with external distractions all the time. Let's understand this a little more.

Imagine our mind to be like a child who is busy playing on the ground. The child falls and hurts the knee, but continues to play without paying attention to the hurt. When the child doesn't pay attention, the experience of pain goes away for a short while, but the hurt still exists. Let's say the child keeps playing and gets some more scratches and cuts. Even now the child continues to play without paying heed to the hurt. Now there will be a time when the pain from those hurts will be quite severe. And because they have not been taken care of, the hurt may continue to grow deeper.

This is exactly what has happened to us. When there is some situation that creates some form of suffering (mental pain), and we do not take time to heal it. Inner wounds continued to grow till the time it got so deep that today we are not even able to look at the wounds. These wounds may be of this lifetime or from our past life. Imagine how much burden of hurt and suffering is being carried, without even being aware.

The mind keeps taking us back to past situations where hurt was created and not healed. That is the mind's way of expressing the hurt.

Even if you wonder why sometimes there is anxiety associated with the future. Possibly because there are these memories of the experience of past hurt and there is fear that the future does not bring those hurtful past experiences in the future. If past suffering is healed, chances are that our future fears will also tend to diminish.

Most of us do not create the future, we re-create the past in our future by not healing the past hurt. This is the reason why certain types of situations come to us repeatedly. If you do not want to re-create the past in the future, then heal it now.

The way to our suffering and also the way out of our suffering is through our thoughts.

The Journey of Thoughts to Experience

Our every thought could be a source of our suffering or healing, depending on the quality of our thoughts. Let's understand this a bit more.

Our every thought creates our feelings and our feelings become the experience of our life.

Let's understand this using a simple example: In whatever situation you are in, at the moment, create below given thought.

> **Thought 1**: I am stressed today
> **Feeling:** Stress
> **Experience:** Stressful

> **Thought 2**: I am calm and relaxed
> **Feeling:** Calm, relaxed
> **Experience:** Calmness

In the above example, the situation was the same. However, the choice of thought was different and your experience of that moment changed. This is how powerful our thoughts are.

Repeated thoughts of hurt and suffering create unhappy experiences in our lives. Repeated thoughts of healing create healing and happiness.

Becoming Aware of Thoughts

Most of the humans today are operating out of unconscious thinking where they are not even aware that they are creating hurtful thoughts. And so, suffering and unhappiness almost look like inseparable parts of our existence.

But let me reaffirm that there is a way out of unconscious thinking and unhappiness.

One simple practice that can help you get over the unconscious thinking pattern is **"Watching the Thoughts"**. Let us understand this in detail.

Watch Your Thoughts Exercise

Step 1 — Listen to the voice of your thoughts as an observer

Step 2 — Observe the emotions that the thoughts are creating

Step 3 — Do not resist or judge your thoughts, just observe

Step 4 — Pay attention to repeated thoughts and emotions

When you practice this exercise, YOU become the listener of your inner voice and in this state, you can have realisation of your own presence which is separate from your thoughts and emotions.

Caution while practicing this exercise: watch your thoughts non-judgmentally and as an observer so that you do not get carried away by emotions.

Our Inner World

Today we are aware of everything that happens in the outside world. But hardly aware of our inner environment. It is a good practice to pause in between for a few moments and check the weather of our inner world.

> Make it a habit to pause and observe your thoughts and emotions.
>
> Ask yourself how is the environment in my inner world.

Our inner world is made up of our thoughts and feelings.

The easiest way to do that is by deeply reflecting on certain questions given below, but not looking for an answer. Just reflect and feel.

1. What is going on inside me?
2. Am I at ease at this moment?
3. How is my body responding to what's going on in my inside world?

When you become an observer of your thoughts and emotions, you awaken an inner dimension of the self that is beneath the thoughts.

In the conscious presence of who you are, thoughts and emotions slowly subside as you are no longer one with your thoughts. Your original self emerges from the realm of your thoughts.

This enables experiencing life not just through the dimension of mind, but experiencing life fully.

Inner Dialogue

Inner Dialogue is also called Self-Talk. It is the conversation that we have with ourselves. This conversation is in the form of an almost uninterrupted stream of thoughts. It is the inner voice that is based on your beliefs and preferences about yourself and your life.

Our inner dialogue forms the basis of our self-esteem. It is a good practice to observe your inner dialogue every day for a few minutes. How do you talk to yourself, how do you talk about your life? Every time there is some challenging situation, how do you take care of your mental health?

Imagine a friend, who may be going through some tough time in life, what would you say to your friend -would you rather say –

- ✓ Don't worry, it will be okay.
- ✓ I am with you, we will sail through this.
- ✓ You will manage this situation well.
- ✓ Don't give up.
- ✓ Life's ups and downs are temporary. This too shall pass.

Now ask yourself, do you say this to yourself in challenging times? Or do you create panic, sadness, anger, or any other negative emotion that makes your inner state even more vulnerable?

A deep belief that we carry, when we get upset is - everything outside should happen as per what we think is right. And when situations or people turn out to be different, we feel upset about it.

It is not the situation or behaviour of people that creates disturbance in our inner world, but our belief that everything will happen according to our will, that creates disturbance.

Situations are just external realities and do not create our thoughts or responses. Our state of acceptance or non-acceptance creates our thoughts and responses.

All of us are experienced enough in life that people and situations are not in our control. Yet, this deep belief system plays its role and creates disturbance in our inner world when external realities of life are not according to our will.

Check your inner dialogue about yourself and your life situations. Do you ever say this to yourself:

➢ Why am I like this?
➢ I wish I was better at something.
➢ How could this happen to me?
➢ Why does he behave like this with me?
➢ Why did they say this to me?

These are all statements indicating the subtle need to control external situations. If your inner dialogue is full of these statements. Let's bring about a small shift.

Let's shift from 3 Cs to 3As.

Criticism	Appreciation
Complaint	Approval
Comparison	Acceptance

Every time you observe your inner dialogue revolves around any of the 3 Cs. Pause and Transform it to 3 As. The more you practice 3 A's in life, the more you will be at ease in life.

Think-A-Thon

- Our every thought creates our feeling and our feeling becomes the experience of our life.

- The moment you choose different thoughts – feelings change – and your experience of life changes in that moment. This is the power of our thoughts.

- When you become the listener of your inner voice, in this state you can have realisation of your own presence which is separate from your thoughts and emotions.

- Your inner world is made up of your thoughts and feelings.

- When you become an observer of your thoughts and emotions, you awaken an inner dimension of the self that is beneath the thoughts.

- In the conscious presence of who you are, thoughts and emotions slowly subside as you are no longer one with your thoughts. Your original self emerges from the realm of your thoughts.

4. Pain and Suffering

Reflection Exercise:

1. Pain and Suffering: is the meaning of these 2 words the same or different?

   _____

2. What is your understanding of these words?
   a. Pain

   _____
   _____

   b. Suffering

   _____
   _____

3. What causes you pain/suffering?

   _____
   _____
   _____

4. Who is responsible for your pain/suffering in life?

   _____
   _____
   _____

Let's start with understanding what we mean by pain and suffering. Does pain and suffering have the same meaning, or are they different?

Well, the dictionary meaning of pain is physical discomfort caused by illness or injury. However, suffering mostly refers to the mental state of enduring the pain or sadness. So, despite pain and suffering being used as synonyms, technically, both are different.

In this chapter, we are looking at these terms (pain and suffering) in their literal sense to help you understand how to overcome mental suffering (hereafter in this chapter referred to as suffering).

To simplify it further, let us understand pain as pain or ache in the physical body and suffering as mental and emotional suffering.

Example: When 2 patients see a doctor for the same illness with a similar degree of physical discomfort, not necessarily both of them suffer equally. You may see one suffering by constantly talking about the illness and how it has made his/her life miserable and another patient may be smiling and exhibiting positivity despite the physical discomfort.

This example helps us understand that the physical condition of illness may or may not be in our control, but suffering definitely is. Suffering is due to our mental response to either physical pain or any external situation that is not in our favour. Feelings and emotions that we experience are the result of our mental response.

Pain is inevitable, but not Suffering from Pain

In today's world where illnesses and diseases are prevailing, pain may be inevitable, however suffering due to pain definitely can be avoided or reduced to a certain degree. Let us see how to reduce this form of suffering.

When patients who are able to remain happy even in terminal illnesses are observed, there are few common attributes that are associated with them:

1. The first one is – the ability to live life in the present. When there are thoughts about how life was better in the past before the illness or how life will turn out to be after the illness and treatment can be quite stressful. Hence living in the present and focusing on healing is very essential.

2. Looking at positives - even when you have to look a little harder. All of us have experienced life enough to know that life does have its share of challenging times, especially when someone is going through illness. However, even at such times, when a person is able to find and look at blessings like support from family and friends, timely and appropriate treatment being received, or any such blessing, chances of being happy and reducing suffering even in times of pain, is much higher.

3. Resilience – is the ability to not give up and keep going despite challenges.

4. Faith – in the presence of divine power, the Supreme always being there with them at every step.

It has been observed that people who imbibe the qualities and attributes mentioned above, not only suffer less in pain but also respond better to treatment and heal faster.

Suffering – the creation of the mind

Let us now deep-dive into how suffering is created and what can we do to end suffering, or at least reduce the experience of it. Suffering is the mind's resistance to everything that was, is, or imagined to be. Resistance creates suffering. The intensity of the suffering depends on the intensity of resistance. Resistance is a form of judgment of what should be and should not be.

The most important thing to understand here is, the energy of resistance never changes our situation. It only makes the situation look bigger than what it is. The energy of resistance just creates more suffering than the situation itself creates.

Resisting past is in the form of below thoughts:

A very important question to ask yourself about the past is: Will resistance in the form of these thoughts change the past?

It is not going to, so why create the suffering?

One of the simplest ways to let the past be past – is by living in the present and not living in the stories of the mind about the past. There may still be times when you would look at yourself getting lost in the stories of past situations. Every time you see yourself doing that, gently and lovingly bring yourself back to the current reality. Practice being in the moment, till it becomes natural to live life like that. Creating suffering from the past situation again in the present and bringing it into the present is a sure way to deepen the wound. Healing happens when you do not create past suffering again on the screen of your mind.

As it is, the past situation is gone, it is no longer our reality, except in our mind. When we replay the past situation repeatedly on the screen of our mind, we are making that our reality of the present in our mind. Today, pause and ask yourself, is it worth creating unpleasant experiences of the past again and again?

One important thing to note here, in the past when that situation might have happened, there may have been multiple factors and people involved that contributed to the existence of that situation. However, today when you are creating it in your mind, you are the only one who  is responsible for it, no one else. Every time you create the past situation on the screen of your mind, every time you repeat the past, you are being unfair to yourself by creating your own suffering, no one else is. Believe me, it is not worth the pain.

Instead, a little effort to let go of the past and being in the present moment is all that it takes to be at ease and experience calmness.

Similarly, there are times when you may see yourself resisting the present. When you are unwilling to do what you need to do in the present or do it unwillingly, you are resisting the present. Example: unwilling to go to work on Monday morning.

And then there are many more ways to resist the future. We do this by assuming or imagining how future situations will turn out to be. Most of the time, we create fear or anxiety hoping that everything falls in place and nothing goes wrong.

By doing this, we are fighting what doesn't even exist and are not sure if it will ever exist, except in our minds.

This is how living in our mind creates stories, which are only illusions, and may or may not ever become a reality.

Well, we can work on everything that is a reality, to make it better. But how can we work on something which does not even exist? This is what creates more fear and feelings of helplessness. Unknowingly, we push ourselves into the darkness of illusion from unreal fearful stories of the mind.

There are 2 ways to deal with fear and anxiety related to the future.

1. Being hopeful – planning for what needs to be done for a better future is necessary. Also, preparing for anything that may not go as per your plan, is also required.

   While we are doing so, we have a choice between 2 types of thoughts:

   i. What if things go wrong?

   ii. What if things go right?

   You have anyways not seen the future, so either of the above thoughts are only thoughts and not reality. Ask yourself what makes you feel at ease. Instead of creating mind stories that are full of distress and hopelessness, be hopeful that with the right state of mind and the right effort, things will turn out to be better.

2. Deal with the future when it is real:

   Each one of us has the power to face life situations when they are there in front of us.

Think of one challenging life situation.

It could be some financial condition, health issue, relationship issue, or any other hard time that you have faced in life.

You have faced that situation and have come out of it!

Similarly, you have the power to deal with everything that life throws at you in the form of situations.

While facing situations, we have a choice of 2 types of thoughts:

Choice 1: How will I face it or deal with it?

Choice 2: I have the power to deal with any situation that comes up.

Both of these are only thoughts. Ask yourself how your state of mind changes in each of these thoughts.

Choice 1: One makes you feel discouraged and disempowered

Choice 2: Makes you feel empowered and hopeful

This technique of choosing the right type of thought will also help you deal with life situations that you are going through, instead of creating suffering.

What if the Present Situation of Life is Unacceptable?

Sometimes people do ask a question: what if the present is unpleasant and unacceptable, is it not better to live in the past or future, at least we can find happiness and hope there.

This question is usually asked by people who are going through situations like the death of a loved one, terminal illness, divorce, etc. where the present seems more difficult.

If you are currently thinking about this, let me ask you a question – avoiding the present, however unacceptable it may seem, may not take away the situation. The situation still exists, you still have to deal with it. Avoiding only creates an illusion that it does not exist which is momentary as ultimately you will have to face it. It is better to face what is real instead of living in an illusion of what is not real as the illusion will sooner or later fall apart in the face of reality.

Once you decide to not avoid the present, the way to deal with suffering is by not labelling situations as tough, challenging, difficult, or unacceptable. Just look at the situation as a reality, without being judgemental about it. By doing this you melt down the resistance toward what is real and you can look at the situation objectively. This will enable you to make right decisions and take appropriate steps to deal with the situation.

Forgiveness

One way of non-acceptance is the inability to forgive which leads to suffering. It is usually in the form of emotions such as blame, resentment, and self-pity. Non-forgiveness could be toward another person or yourself or towards any situation in the past, present, or future – that you resist and deny to accept. However, more commonly it is towards another person.

Forgiveness is a gift you give to others but reap the benefits of it yourself. Forgiveness is a state of complete acceptance where you allow the "is-ness" of what is real and do not create a feeling of resistance.

Forgiveness Exercise:

> Sit in silence for a few moments. Imagine a stage in front of you. In your mind, bring that person on the stage for you may have some form of non-forgiveness. Imagine there is a spotlight on that person.
>
> Look into the eyes of the person and say – I forgive you and let go of my inner resistance. I set you free. I set myself free.
>
> Feel that the person is being blessed with a lot of happiness.

Practice this forgiveness exercise every time you feel there is a need to forgive someone. If the hurt is deep, initially it may be difficult to complete this exercise. But continue to do it till you free yourself from hurt. When you are comfortable to see them smiling and happy, know the healing has happened. You have forgiven. Till then, practice this exercise. Deeper the pain, deeper the practice of forgiveness is required to free yourself from pain.

Always remember, non-forgiveness is like a painful cage you create around yourself, the key to opening the cage is with yourself. So choose forgiveness and set yourself free.

Exercise on Embracing the Present Fully:

A simple, yet powerful exercise to be in the moment and be able to live it intensely is given below. For a couple of moments, leave everything that you are doing aside. Read and experience each line below fully and completely.

"Look around and be where you are. Use your senses to feel everything that is there around you – what you see, what you hear, what you touch..

Don't interpret or judge, just look very deeply.

In the deep stillness of the mind, you hear the sound of the breeze or any other unnoticed sounds present in the place.

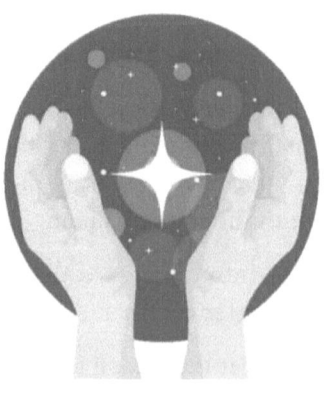

Feel the stillness of your mind connecting to the stillness of things around you.

Observe your breath and follow the natural rhythm of your breath.

Breathing in and out. Feel the air flowing in and out.. allow everything inside and outside to be.

Allow what is inside and outside you.. be completely still and present.

Embrace the present moment fully and completely."

> **Think-A-Thon**
>
> - ❖ Pain is inevitable, but not Suffering from Pain.
> - ❖ Suffering is nothing but the creation of the mind.
> - ❖ Resistance creates suffering. The intensity of the suffering depends on the intensity of resistance. Resistance is a form of judgment of what should be and should not be.
> - ❖ Overcoming resistance to past, present and future is a way to overcome suffering.

5. Ways to deal with Stories of the Mind

Reflection Exercise:

1. Tick the sentences that you think are relevant to you in your life.

   ☐ i. Their behaviour makes me angry.

   ☐ ii. I am feeling low because nothing is working out for me.

   ☐ iii. I am feeling stressed because the situation is quite tough.

   ☐ iv. I am feeling hurt because they betrayed me.

2. Are situations or people responsible for your emotions and experience of life?

   _____
   _____

3. Are there any factors apart from situation and people, that are responsible for your emotions and experiences of life?

   _____
   _____

4. List down situations or people for whom you may be creating energy of resistance.

   (Example: why did this happen to me? Or why they are the way they are?

   _____

   _____

Most people today end up living their lives in their minds and the stories of the mind instead of living life in reality. Constant thoughts on the screen of the mind make people get lost in thoughts of the mind and not experience life where it is happening. There is an almost uninterrupted flow of thoughts which clouds our consciousness.

Let's assume this flow of unconscious thoughts as no light or state of darkness, and aware living as light. You can't fight darkness or no light, you just need to switch on the light.

Let's look at some ways to enable you to come out of this no-light state, by switching on the light of pure and positive thoughts.

From Blame to Responsibility

Shifting from blame to responsibility may be a bit hard if for long you have held others responsible for how you feel. Some of you may also ask – how can I be responsible for all my emotions and experiences,

- after all it is their behaviour that was incorrect which made me feel angry or

- it is the situation that is so tough at this time which makes me feel stressed.

Well, let's understand this a bit more.

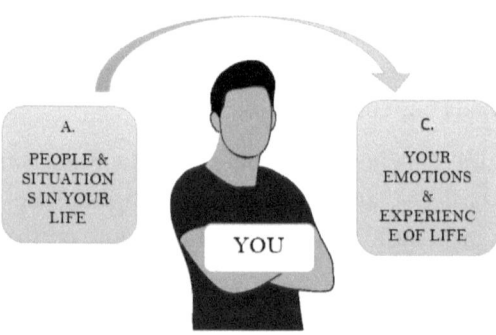

In the above visual, is A directly proportional to C, or is there a missing factor here?

Let's do one simple exercise to understand this.

Attention Exercise

Step 1: Look around and count the number of things that you don't like in that place. You have 15 seconds to count.

Write the number here: ____

Step 2: Look around and count the number of things that you like in that place. You have 15 seconds to count.

Write the number here: ____

Think about it, you are in the same place, and you had the same duration (15 seconds) to complete steps 1 and 2. However, what you chose to see was different in both cases.

This is called attention. Attention is like a focus light -- the focused thought energy directed towards something.

In life, we may not have the option of choosing situations that come up or other people's behaviour, however, it is definitely in our hands where we choose to focus our attention.

That is the missing factor – B. Attention

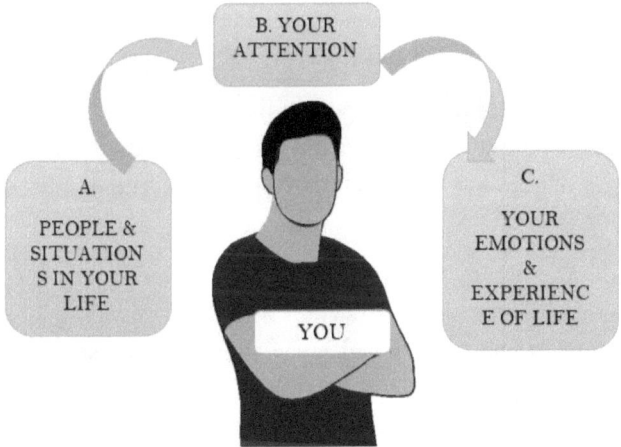

Living in the same life situations and with the same set of people, our experiences are determined by where we choose to focus or what we choose to focus our attention on.

Example 1: A person may have many habits or personality traits. If you focus on the ones that make you feel uncomfortable, you will find them irritating. So it is not they, who create your irritation, it is your attention that creates your irritation.

Example 2: A family may be going through some financial crises. Each family member, even 2 siblings of similar age and upbringing may respond to the situation differently. One sibling may get into deep sorrow, another may pull up his or her socks and take up a job to support the family in times of crisis.

If it was the situation that determined their emotions, both siblings should have had the same emotions, because the situation was the same. However, it is this additional factor that makes all the difference. Our experience of the entire day depends on what we choose to focus on. If we choose to focus on our blessings, we experience calmness and joy.

Attention is our thought energy directed towards something, which creates our response.

To shift from blame to responsibility, instead of focusing our attention on external factors like people and situations (which are not in our control), it is important to focus on our response (which is in our control).

When we blame, we give away our power to choose our response to external factors. This is the easiest way to lose our happiness as at an external level, there may be some or the other things that may not be right as per your perception of right.

Taking responsibility simply means our **Ability to Respond** to a particular situation or behaviour of a person. Our response is generated in our mind which then results in our feelings, emotions, words, and actions.

As a first step towards shifting from blame to taking responsibility, let's take accountability for our experience. Let's understand this with the below examples.

Situation	Blame	Taking Responsibility
Their behaviour	makes me angry	I am creating angry thoughts as a response to their behaviour.
Nothing is working out for me	so I am feeling low	I am creating low-energy thoughts as my response to the situation.
The situation is quite tough	I am stressed because of the situation	I am creating my stress.
They betrayed me	I am hurt because of them	They choose their actions. I am creating my hurt.

Now that you have taken responsibility for your experience, it brings back our power and ability to choose our response. Let's shift to a new way of responding to situations and change our experience of life.

Situation	Taking Responsibility	A New Way of Responding
Their behaviour	I am creating angry thoughts as a response to their behaviour.	I choose to create calm, composed thoughts.
Nothing is working out for me	I am creating low-energy thoughts as my response to the situation.	I will not give up and keep giving my best.
The situation is quite tough	I am creating my stress.	I have enough power to sail through the situation.
They betrayed me	They choose their actions. I am creating my hurt.	I forgive them. I heal myself and experience peace within.

What you think, is how you feel. How you feel, creates your experiences of life.

Our thoughts, however, can be in the form of reaction (automated) or response (consciously chosen thoughts). When we pause and choose the right thought, we tend to create better experiences for ourselves and others around us.

When we practice this, pause and choose the right thought, we become the master of our own thoughts and feelings. Instead of allowing thoughts and feelings to become our master and lead us nowhere.

Follow below given simple steps to practice "pause and choose your response".

Step 1: Shift from blame (on situation or people) to responsibility – know that your emotions are your own creation basis the thoughts you create.

Step 2: In any situation, pause – choose the right thought of acceptance, patience, kindness, compassion, and joy.

Step 3: Experience positive feelings generated by creating the right thought.

Our thoughts give rise to our feelings, our feelings lead to our experiences. If someday, you are not feeling good, do not try to change your feelings, instead observe what thoughts are creating the feelings and thus change the thoughts. The below table will make this even more clear.

Thought	Feeling
I am a happy person.	Happiness
Why is my life like this?	Dissatisfaction
I am a peaceful being.	Peace
My life is full of chaos and stressful situations	Chaos and Stress
I accept them as they are.	Calmness
Why don't they change?	Dislike towards them
I forgive them.	Freedom from suffering
Why did they do this to me?	Hurt

So, the quality of our life experiences depends on the quality of our thoughts.

Acceptance and Gratitude

Another very important aspect of learning to deal with the stories of mind is Acceptance and Gratitude. Have you observed how someone can stay calm and positive in the toughest of situations and someone can pick and find negatives even in a perfect situation?

Let's engage in the below exercise to talk about both in detail.

Look at the below box for 5 seconds.

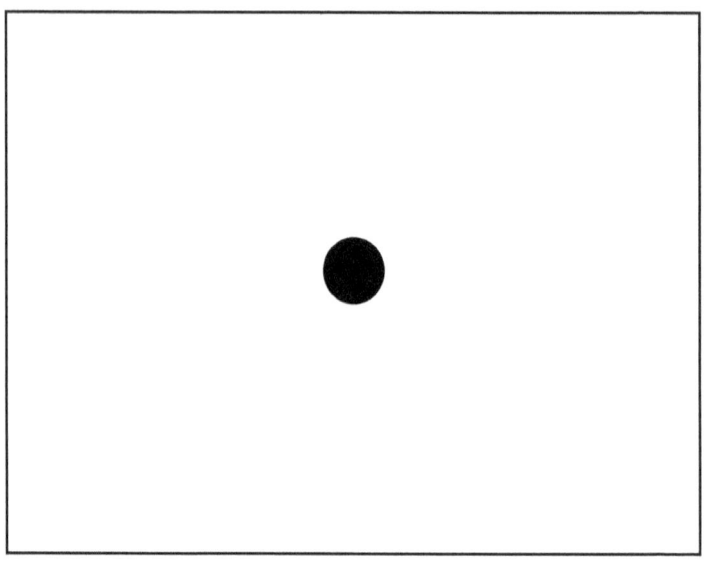

What did you see inside the box?

_____

Most of the responses received when this question is asked - a black dot. Did you also look at the black dot inside the box?

There are also a few responses like a black dot in white space.

Now, ask yourself, why did you see what you saw?

This box is like our life. Our life may have a lot of white spaces and some black dots too. White spaces are good things in life like our parents, friends, family, education, career, or any other aspect of life that you may consider a blessing. The black dot represents some situations or experiences that may have been tough or uncalled for.

Write down 5 blessings of your life in below box:

```
Box 1

1. _____

2. _____

3. _____

4. _____

5. _____
```

Write Down some of the challenges or uncalled-for situations of your life in the box below:

```
Box 2

1. _____

2. _____

3. _____
```

Now ask yourself how much of your mental energy is invested in Box 1 versus Box 2.

For Box 1: The more you think about your blessings, the more at peace and happy you will be in life.

Thinking about blessings creates a feeling of gratitude. Make sure to spend some time every day reminding yourself of your blessings. Morning, when you wake up, remind yourself how blessed you are for all the good things you have in your life.

Let us also understand what we do with the black dots of our lives. Well, resisting the black dots by saying 'Why did this happen to me?' or 'Why they are the way they are?' doesn't change the situation. It only disturbs our mental state. To overcome the energy of resistance, create a thought of acceptance. Be it people or situations. Let's look at the above list of black dots that you have written.

Take them one by one. Look at each one in your mind's eye and say to yourself – I accept it as it is / I accept them as they are. Create a feeling of deep and complete acceptance.

Whatever is your current reality, accept it as if you had chosen it. Work along with it, not against it. Acceptance will completely shift and transform your energy level.

Once there is complete acceptance in the mind, you will experience stability of mind. With this state of mind and calmness within– work towards the external realities and do everything to make the situation better at an external level. But in the process do not lose your calmness by resistance. Resistance doesn't make things better. A calm and stable mind does.

Remember blessings attract more blessings. Sending out the energy of acceptance and gratitude is a way to experience blessings in life.

Think-A-Thon

- Our experience of the entire day, depends on what we choose to focus on. If we choose to focus on our blessings, we experience calmness and joy.

- Attention is basically our thought energy directed towards something, which creates our response.

- Taking responsibility simply means our Ability to Respond to a particular situation or behaviour of a person. Our response is generated in our mind which then results into our feelings, emotions, words, and actions.

- What you think, is how you feel. How you feel, creates your experiences of life.

- Thinking about blessings creates a feeling of gratitude.

- Blessings attract more blessings

6. Relationship Healing

Reflection Exercise:

1. Tick ✓ for statements that are true for you in your relations.
   - [ ] a. I am my best self when I am with my loved ones.
   - [ ] b. I am my worst self when I am with my loved ones.
   - [ ] c. I feel most hurt because of people close to me.
   - [ ] d. I shout and yell most when I am with the person closest to me. I vent my anger on them.

2. Do you think there are moments of hurt and resentment in your relationships with your loved ones? Can you describe a little more about the same?

   _____
   _____
   _____
   _____

3. Do you think there is room for healing relationships with your loved ones? Describe what aspect you want to heal and with whom.

   _____
   _____
   _____
   _____

What needs healing?

Can you do anything to heal a relationship? Well, according to me relationships do not need healing. It is the people who need healing. Once the person is healed – i.e., you are healed, your relationship will heal automatically. Let's understand this equation.

A relationship is nothing but an exchange of energy between two people. The energy we share with people is the energy we create and have within us. Thoughts and feelings are the energy we create and radiate to the world around us.

Circle of Relationships Exercise:

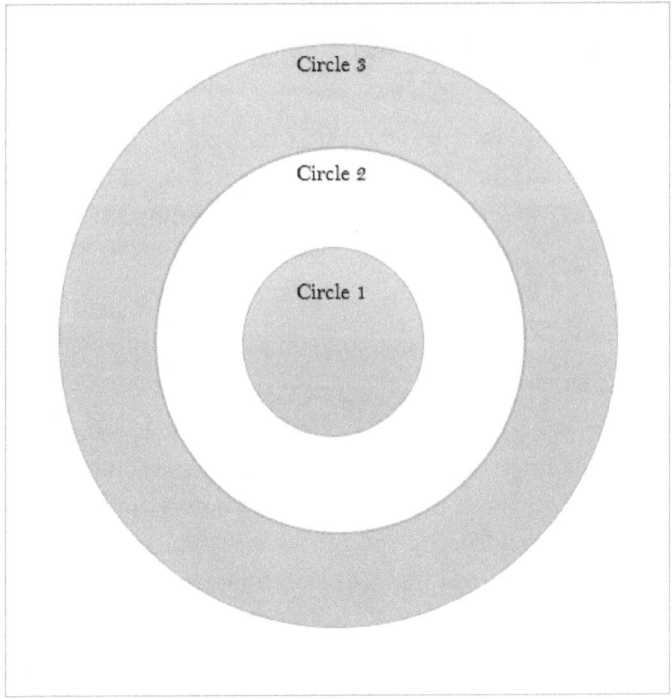

Look at your life and the people around you who matter to you in your life. Write the names of people in the above box as per the below instructions:

Circle 1 (Priority 1): name of a person most dear to you.

Circle 2 (Priority 2): names of 2 people who are dear to you, apart from the name mentioned in Circle 1.

Circle 3 (Priority 3): names of 3 people who are dear to you, apart from 3 names already mentioned in Circles 1 and 2.

Reflection:

Most people end up writing the names of their children, spouse, parents, or friends. Have you also written their names, but forgot to write your own name?

In which circle did your name appear? Did you write your name in any of the circles?

Your relationship with yourself is the energy you create all throughout the day. How you think and feel about yourself (in the context of others) creates hurt or healing within you. Thoughts of judgment and non-acceptance towards self are then carried forward in other relations in the below 2 ways:

1. Either you become judgemental and non-accepting towards others
2. Or your constant energy of judging yourself and not accepting yourself is radiated to people around, and they too see you in the same light as you see yourself. They catch your energy and reflect that same energy to you. Then you feel judged and non-accepted by people around you.

Hence, to a large extent, **our Relationships with other people are a reflection of our relationship with ourselves.**

In either of the above situations, there is the experience of hurt, misunderstanding, resentment, and guilt. All these are the result of energies that humans are creating through their thoughts and emotions.

Working to heal each of the relationships in our life is like watering each leaf whereas water is needed in the roots. Roots are our own thoughts, feelings, and emotions. If the roots are nourished, the entire tree will blossom, but if we forget to nourish the roots and focus on each of the leaves, ultimately the tree will perish. This is what is happening to our relationships today.

There are also a large number of people who are now choosing to live their lives alone, to avoid any experience of rejection or failure in relationships. However, if the mind continues to create the same thoughts, and experience the same emotions, then living with or without other people becomes immaterial as the experience of life may not be different. After all, avoiding something doesn't mean the energy doesn't exist. It still does, in a dormant form, and will become active at the smallest of opportunities.

Relationships – a pathway for realization

Sometimes you may say that people closest to you bring out the worst in you or you feel most hurt by the person you love the most or you get angry with people who are very dear to you. However, nobody can get into your mind and create your thoughts and emotions. They do their action and looking at their action, we create our thoughts and emotions. These thoughts and emotions are in fact pathways for us to understand what inside us needs healing.

If anger is triggered by looking at someone's behaviour, they don't create your anger – it is already within you in a dormant form and becomes active when their action triggers anger.

They do not hurt you, no one can. They only do their action as per what is appropriate for them, looking at their action – the hurt that is already within you gets triggered.

These emotions of hurt, resentment, anger, jealousy, and possessiveness are reflections of emotions created and residing inside you. Every time you recreate it and experience it, you add to your stock of these emotions.

Healing relationships start with healing these emotions that you are carrying for many months, years, or even births.

Here, two aspects are important:

1. Healing past emotional hurt from relationships
2. Not creating new negative emotion

Steps to heal emotions within:

Step 1: Make a note of a few situations that triggered a discomforting emotional reaction.

Step 2: Find a commonality between these situations – person/people or behaviours or any other common aspect.

Step 3: Become aware – awareness of your own patterns and everything that triggers negative emotions in you plays a key role in healing.

Step 4: From blame to accountability – know that it is not because of them or that, it is your pattern that is acting out. Take ownership of your emotions and become in charge of it.

Step 5: Every time the pattern is activated, observe your emotions very deeply. Don't become one with your emotions. Observe it. Become still, fully present, and fully aware.

When you become fully aware, you separate yourself from the stream of emotions. Then emotions slowly subside as it doesn't get your energy and attention any longer.

Here, awareness is the key that creates distance between your emotions and you. And thus, emotions do not get further charged. Once emotions slowly subside, then creating thoughts and feelings that are comforting – acceptance, compassion, etc.

This is the way to withdraw your energy from past hurt and not create further hurt. But this requires practice, intense intention of healing, and patience with yourself. There may be times when you still end up reacting to your loved ones. But that's exactly an indication that the practice needs to be deepened. The more the intensity of practice, the more the healing.

Your healing – may help them heal

Once you start your healing journey and have walked some miles, there may be situations when you are fine but people around you may still be operating out of unconsciousness – their hurt, resentment, insecurities, etc. There may be situations when their unconscious behaviour triggers unconsciousness in you too! Understand once again – that your healing process is still a work in progress.

When you operate out of consciousness and live an aware life – and see your loved ones continuing to live in emotional pain, you no longer absorb their negativity. You see the pain in their behaviour and so do not create hurt, anger, or irritation. You continue to remain aware and in light of peace and positivity. Your light of peace and positivity might bring light to them if they choose to allow that light within them. Now they may start absorbing your light of consciousness and that may help them come out of their unconscious patterns of hurt, resentment, anger, etc. But ultimately their healing is their choice. You can only provide them light, walking in light or moving deeper into darkness is a choice that each person makes for themselves. In any case, you no longer add to your emotional pain and also bring light to everyone around.

When you give light, your own light Grows

Whatever you give to others, you are the first one to receive. When you get angry at someone, you are the first one to experience it. They may absorb your energy of anger or choose to ignore it, depending on their patterns. However, one person to get it for sure, is you yourself. Similarly, when you radiate the light of peace, positivity, love, and joy to others, you experience it first. When you experience the light within you, the light grows within you.

So, whether they choose consciousness or not, you continue to grow in your journey towards enlightenment when you give light and become full of light.

You give what you have!

When you have anger, frustration, and resentment inside, you do not need to make an effort to give that to people. You end up giving them the same through your vibrations, words, and actions. Similarly, when you are healed and conscious, you need not make an effort to give it to others, you radiate peace, positivity, and empowering vibrations to everyone.

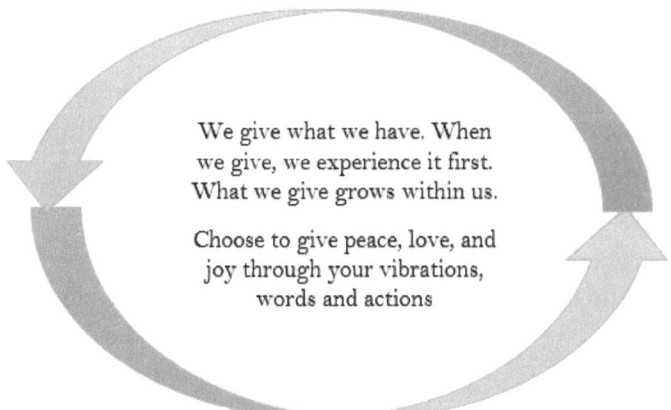

We give what we have. When we give, we experience it first. What we give grows within us.

Choose to give peace, love, and joy through your vibrations, words and actions

So let's take some moments here to reflect: what do people around you experience with you, from you? That is what is there within you. Ask yourself what you want to give to them (peace? Love? Happiness?) and create what you wish to give to your loved ones.

Thoughts – basis of Healing

When we learn to create the right thoughts and feelings for everyone around us, irrespective of their behaviour, healing happens. Our thoughts become a source of healing instead of a source of hurt for ourselves and others.

The Doer and the Doing

If some change in the behaviour of our loved ones is required (for example - a child throwing tantrums or a spouse getting angry and hurt), you continue to guide and instruct them, but not with the energy of rejecting them for their behaviour. You see the doings separate from the doer. You know the person is a pure being and just has the colour of these negative emotions on them. When you are conscious and aware, you are able to separate the person from their momentary negative emotions and behaviours.

You continue to have love and respect for the being while helping them to realise their behaviour that needs attention or change.

At the workplace, if you have a difference of opinion with a colleague or team member, you continue to have regard for them and operate from the mindset that you have a difference in opinion or idea, but not a difference with the person. Then the level of conversation with people around goes to a different dimension. Conversations still happen, and differences still crop up, but regard continues to be there between people.

Being Connections

Connections deepen when we connect with the being instead of their name, position, attire, looks, behaviour. Think about it, when we are talking to someone, are we talking to the being, or are we talking to their external possessions or acquired personality?

Example: When you enter a bank for some bank transaction, you meet a security person, then the receptionist, then the bank employee who would help you with your transaction, and finally the branch head. Ask yourself does your mental response and behaviour change with each one basis role and your requirements. If it does, then chances are you are interacting with a role or position instead of the being.

When you talk to someone or are listening to another person, don't just listen with your mind, listen with your complete being. Give them your complete attention. Be aware of your own energy field and how it is responding to what they are saying. This also awakens the realisation of being in them, to the degree they allow it to. Relationships can turn into a spiritual practice in this way. Being in touch with your own inner self creates a clear space within which the relationship can flourish.

From seeker to giver in relationship

Today, everyone is seeking love, happiness, and peace from others. Everyone who feels incomplete within is seeking from others. There is a complete cycle of expectations and disappointments in relations.

This reminds me of a story of a beggar who was sitting on a wooden box asking passers-by for some money. For years he has been sitting in the same place on the same wooden box asking for money. One day a passer-by did not have enough money to give, but asked him if he had ever opened the wooden box and seen what was inside the box. Well, to the beggar's surprise, when he opened the box, it was full of money and jewels.

You may have heard this story before. This story is an attempt to remind you of the treasures that are there within you.

This story is of everyone who is seeking from others. They are not aware that they are themselves the treasure house of everything that they are seeking. It is only about becoming aware of their inner wealth of peace, love, and happiness. Once they become aware, they feel full and complete within.

Then the repeated cycle of expectations (from others) and disappointment (when you do not get from them) ends. A new dimension opens up in relationships. Where we move from seeking to offering. You have enough within to be able to offer without any expectations because when you are full inside you don't seek a sense of fulfilment and completeness from relations.

Connecting with the Higher Source

In your journey, at any point, if you feel you do not have enough love or joy or peace and feel a need for someone to bestow you with these in the form of blessings; just look above and have faith in the Supreme, the source of peace, love, and joy.

You may name the Supreme differently, but the ultimate bestower of all that you seek is just a thought away. One honest thought of remembrance of the Supreme and you can experience God's canopy of peace, love, and happiness around you.

> **Think-A-Thon**
>
> ❖ Relationships do not need healing. It is the people who need healing
>
> ❖ Relationship is an exchange of energy between two people. The energy we share with people, is the energy we create and have within us.
>
> ❖ Thoughts and feelings are the energy we create and radiate to the world around us.
>
> ❖ Relationships with other people are a reflection of our relationship with ourselves.
>
> ❖ We give what we have. When we give, we experience it first. What we give grows within us.
>
> ❖ One honest thought of remembrance of the Supreme and you can experience God's canopy of peace, love, and happiness around you.

7. Ego Identification

Reflection Exercise:

1. Do you feel good when someone appreciates you?
   ☐ Yes   ☐ No

2. Do you feel disturbed when some comments on your attire or work that you have done?
   ☐ Yes   ☐ No

3. Do you feel your mood going up and down based on what people around you say to you?
   ☐ Yes   ☐ No

4. Do you feel a sudden shift of mood for no apparent reason?
   ☐ Yes   ☐ No

5. Do you feel you sometimes lose your sense of self and get totally identified with your role or your relationships (boss, team member, parent, partner, child) that it takes your complete attention? Describe such roles and relationships.

   _____
   _____
   _____
   _____

Faces of Ego

The ego is defined in different ways by different people. Simply put, Ego can be described as the false identification to something that you are not.

Example: In a business meeting, you propose an idea. The idea is opposed by another colleague who had come up with a different plan.

Response 1:

Let me understand what he is proposing. And choose what is best for the organisation.

Response 2:

How can he negate my idea? I have been managing this business for a much longer time. He is new to this department and thinks too much about himself.

Get into an argument with the colleague and ask your colleague to keep out of this.

Response 2 typically shows deep identification with an idea. A little threat to an idea becomes a threat to your own identity. Your idea becomes your ego identity.

This is how the ego operates. The ego operates from a dysfunctional mindset of win-lose and is driven by fear and insecurity.

Similarly, you could be attached to your looks, your attire, your relations, your role, your religion, nationality, or gender.

Example: you are deeply identified with your role as a mother so much that you have lost yourself in that role of a mother.

Now, imagine a situation where your child does not reciprocate to your love and disrespects you or chooses someone else over you. How would you feel at that time?

Would you feel your entire world is shattered and there is nothing to look forward to in life?

Or if someone makes a passing comment that your neighbour takes care of her children better and how their children are well behaved. What will be your response to that person? Would it hurt?

Since the ego is driven by fear, a person who lives in ego identity always experiences emotional vulnerability. You cannot be stable and at ease, as your sense of identity is based on false identification and so can be threatened.

Have you experienced this – if someone appreciates, you feel elevated? If someone criticizes you, you feel low and disturbed.

You would say – is it not natural to feel good when someone appreciates you? Well, then we must also accept that our life experiences will then be like a swing that keeps going up and down. If, in appreciation, you feel good, then in criticism, you are bound to feel disturbed because your sense of self is attached to others' opinion of you.

It is not necessary that everyone would approve of your decisions, choices, and ways of living. Understanding that people may have their opinions and you can't stop others from expressing their views. However, if you are identified with something that they have a different view about, it will disturb you and also your future conversation with that person. Now that doesn't seem like a very healthy way of living.

Ego also leads to a feeling of superiority or inferiority which takes us away from the real identification of the Self. It is important to understand that if you are superior to person X, there will also be person Y, who may be superior to you in some or the other aspect. A feeling of superiority or inferiority only creates disturbance as both of these are ego identities and can be threatened or challenged.

Orbit of your life

We also get identified with the messages we have received from our parents, teachers, and friends when we are growing up. The messages become our identity in our minds as we grow up.

These messages could be (in expressed or form of Subtle cues)–

- ➢ You are not strong enough
- ➢ You are not good enough,
- ➢ You are not loved enough
- ➢ Your opinion does not matter.

Different people pick up different messages in their childhood and make these messages their self-identity.

As a person grows up, this disempowering belief system about the self has an impact on their self-esteem and their communication and connections with people.

For example: a person who has a belief that "I am not good enough – will either try to prove to the world that he or she is very good, or live a mediocre life, believing they are not good enough.

If a person has a belief that "I am not lovable or loved enough", he or she constantly seeks attention and needs validation from their loved ones about being loved.

If a person has picked up a belief that "I am not strong enough or I am weak" will either try and hide that from the world and build physical strength and muscles and do everything to negate that belief; or will make weakness their identity.

Different people pick up different messages and make them their identity and may have different ways of dealing with it – either by proving to the world that it is not true or making it their personality. Either of the responses is not healthy as it makes you emotionally vulnerable and seek validation from people around you.

Most people are not even aware of their disempowering belief system around which their entire life revolves like an orbit. These beliefs about the self are very deep and subtle and form a part of their subconscious or unconscious personality. What one can only see is a person's external reaction in the form of an emotional outburst as an external manifestation of the inner belief.

However, such belief systems can be identified and worked upon with deep observation and awareness.

Follow the below steps to identify your orbit.

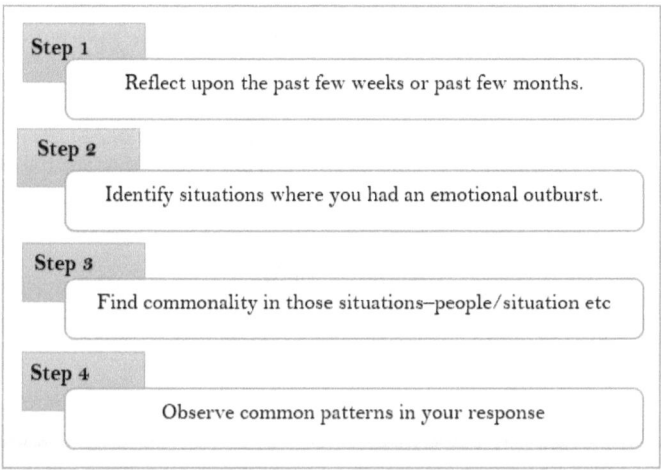

Step 1 Reflect upon the past few weeks or past few months.

Step 2 Identify situations where you had an emotional outburst.

Step 3 Find commonality in those situations—people/situation etc

Step 4 Observe common patterns in your response

The above steps will enable you to pick up your repeated thought behaviour pattern. This thought behaviour pattern is an indication of what creates a disturbance in your mental state time and again.

Once you have identified your pattern, follow the below steps to identify your core belief about yourself.

Basis the common aspects in the above situations, ask yourself what triggers your emotional outburst. What emotions do you experience and what are you seeking in that moment?

To identify your orbit, write 'x' and 'y' in the below box, basis statements/situations that trigger your emotional outburst. If someone said this to you or made you feel this way, you would end up losing your temper and react.

> I am too 'X'
>
> 1. _____
> 2. _____
>
> I am not enough 'Y'
>
> 1. _____
> 2. _____

Now, for the next couple of weeks validate, which statement out of the statements mentioned by you in the above box triggers your emotional outburst. That is a disempowering belief about yourself that needs healing.

If you haven't been able to identify your orbit yet, nothing to worry about. Keep observing situations where you experience emotional disturbance and understand what validation are you looking for, from people and situations.

Case Study on Overcoming Orbit of Life

Recently, I met a college-going girl who discussed her emotional outbursts over little situations or comments. These emotional outbursts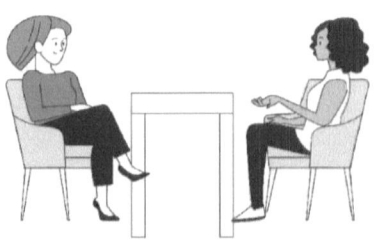

were very frequent (at least once a week) and the intensity of her outbursts was very intense. Every time she would get upset about something; she would react strongly by getting angry at people involved in that situation. Once the situation had passed and her anger subsided, she would keep crying and feel sad about it for days. This had become a routine up-and-down swing of her emotions.

We worked together on this for a few weeks. Every time she got emotionally disturbed, she would talk about how the situation or people were to be blamed for how she was feeling. She would mention everything wrong the person did that created her emotional reaction. Of course, she was also feeling sad about losing her mind every time and reacting in such a strong way.

Through all the conversations we had over 6-7 weeks, I could see she was seeking validation for her being lovable and important.

What I could hear from our conversations is that the moment she felt she was not important, her need for validation for being important or loved was challenged and she would feel extremely upset about it.

What I also noticed along the way is that she was seeking validation to her being important especially when she was around this specific set of people (her very close friend, and everyone who was closely connected to that friend).

One very deep observation that I had throughout the discussion is that – that person would do everything right or almost everything right for her, support her, care, listen to her, etc. but if there is any situation that involves her this friend where she is made to feel ignored, or unattended she would start blaming him and everyone involved in the situation.

So, through all these observations, we could identify that her disempowering belief system was that she was not valuable or important. She kept seeking validation that she was important from the person she values.

When initially, I tried to convince her that it is not the situation or person who is responsible for her feelings, she could just not agree and would give many many reasons to prove it was them. Slowly, when I made her aware of her orbit and how because of her orbit she is not able to see 8 good things that the person has done and focuses on 2 things that may not have gone right. Now as time passed, she started realising, it was not them, but her own orbit that was acting out every time she was getting disturbed. Even then, it wasn't easy for her to overcome her emotional reaction and outburst when the situation came up.

Slowly, by being aware and observing herself during such situations the intensity of her emotional outburst slowly reduced. She also made her friend aware of her orbit and so the friend was also able to help her by going the extra mile and letting her know how important she is.

This to a great extent helped her reduce the intensity of her emotional outburst.

The key here is to shift from blame to realisation – it is not them, it is your own orbit acting out. Every time a situation comes up, just be aware and observe your patterns. Do not get carried away with emotions but become an observer of your thought-behaviour pattern.

When you disidentify from your emotions and become the observer, the emotional energy creating disturbance slowly subsides. Though it will continue to operate for a while and will try to pull you back into the emotional ditch. However, it will subside fully when you are aware and observe. Conscious attention enables the emotional upheaval to subside and settle down.

In this process, it is important to NOT think about it or judge or analyse your emotions. Don't let observation turn into thinking and identifying with the emotions. Stay present, and continue to observe what is happening inside you. Deepen your practice of becoming an observer of your emotions and you will learn to master your emotions.

Life inside-out

Through my journey of observation and awareness, what I have come to realise is – till we overcome deep inner programming of disempowering belief systems, we continue to radiate the same kind of energy through our thinking patterns. Our energy attracts situations and people in our lives. Sometimes, we are not even aware of why we encounter the same kind of experiences, we may change jobs, we may change people, city, or even country; but if we haven't changed our belief systems, we continue to radiate the same energy and attract similar experiences in life.

This also happens, because our energies are received by people around us and bring out similar experiences from them.

I came across a person who was being criticized by most of the people in his life. If he met a person who was not otherwise critical, even that person would start criticizing him. This is because there is a subtle energy that is going out from him which brings out that kind of behaviour in others.

If we work at an inside level and create positive belief systems for ourselves, we will automatically attract positive life situations.

That is why it is said Life is Inside-Out.

Ego Identities Versus Self

As we travel through this human journey, we acquire a lot of false identities such as name, fame, possessions, power, authority, roles, professions, etc. Now the reality is that they are yours but they are not you. You have them, but you are not them. However, in this journey, we get so attached to these labels that instead of living life like Human Beings we start living like Human Doings or Human Possessing.

A Human Being simply means – a Being or an energy on this human journey.

When we are so identified with our role or profession (I am mother, I am Doctor), we become human doing and our entire consciousness strives and thrives on the existence of the role or procession. Well, understanding that I am not a mother or a doctor, I am a Being, doctor is my profession, and mother to child is a role basis the relationship.

Similarly, when your sense of self is derived from things that you have acquired like an expensive car or a lavish house – then we become human possessing instead of human beings.

Now you may ask, what is wrong with getting attached to things that we possess or roles that we play? After all, it is mine. That is the whole point – it is yours, not you. When you are too much identified with externalities of the world, which are temporary – they can be taken away from you or can be destroyed. They are not permanent. Hence there is always a sense of fear and insecurity attached to it. When there is fear and insecurity and if anyone tries to take it away from you or challenge it – it feels as if your whole being is being challenged and thus there is anger, hatred, etc.

Example: You bought your dream car just a week back and you had parked it outside your apartment. Someone accidentally dashes their car against your car and there are scratches on your car. How you get into extreme pain and agony. This is because you are so identified with the car and as if scratches are not on the car but on you.

This doesn't mean we don't take care of things or we don't play our role well. However, when there is clarity of who I am and what is mine, there is a sense of stability in the mind. Then you can take care of everything well and also deal with unforeseen situations like car accidents well without getting emotionally drained by it.

For this, it is important to see yourself as the light or energy within this human body. The light which is self-illuminating and no one can take away. The energy that is ever present and permanent, no one can destroy. In this state, there is no fear of loss or insecurity.

You are whole and complete by yourself and there is nothing to seek from the external world and nothing that anyone can take away from you. After all, no one can take away you from yourself.

This is the real self. And when we operate from this awareness, we can truly cherish all the external realities like name, fame, possessions, profession, role, etc.

When you are not driven by Ego identities of identifying yourself with externalities of life, you live fully, live completely and happiness just is an outcome of your consciousness instead of a temporary acquisition.

Ask yourself – don't you want to live your life like that?

To know, what are the ego identities that you are deeply attached to – just observe – what is it that takes most of your attention and energy. Is it your work, relations, goals, things – whatever it may be, will also be something that can lead to a lot of disturbance in your life.

Whatever you think is the source of your happiness, turns out to be a source of unhappiness – that is the ego identity you are attached to.

Switch from ego identities to conscious living as who you are! A Being on this Human Journey. Remind yourself time and again throughout the day.

Think-A-Thon

- ❖ Ego is the false identification to something that you are not.

- ❖ Ego is driven by fear, a person who lives in ego identity always experiences emotional vulnerability.

- ❖ When you disidentify your emotions and become the observer, the emotional energy creating disturbance slowly subsides.

- ❖ Deepen your practice of becoming an observer of your emotions and you will learn to master your emotions.

- ❖ Our energy attracts situations and people in our lives.

- ❖ Human Being simply means – a Being or an energy on this human journey.

- ❖ See yourself as the light or energy within this human body. Light which is self-illuminating and no one can take away. Energy which is ever present and permanent, no one can destroy. In this state, there is no fear of loss or insecurity.

- ❖ Switch from ego identities to conscious living as who you are!

8. The Being – and its Nature

Exercise 1: Draw a picture / rough sketch of yourself in the box below. You may or may not be an artist and that is okay. It need not be perfect, no one will judge you on your drawing skills, so you can feel free and draw with an open mind.

Exercise 2: Focus your attention on your body. Feel its presence. Do you feel energy flowing in your feet, knees, thighs, hands, arms, in your abdomen, your chest? Can you feel the subtle energy field that pervades the entire body and gives vibrant life to every organ and every cell? Continue to focus on the energy that flows into your entire body. Don't think about it, just feel it.

Ask yourself, what if this entire energy that is being transmitted into every organ of the body is withdrawn? Can you feel it being withdrawn? What remains is a statue made up of 5 elements without life.

Reflection Exercise:

1. In exercise 1, what did you draw? Did you draw the face or your body? Describe your drawing in the below space.

   _____

   _____

   _____

2. Are you this body made up of the 5 elements? Or are you the energy, the life force operating this body? Who are you? Describe your understanding of yourself.

   _____

   _____

   _____

3. What is your experience of yourself? How do you feel or sense yourself?

   _____

   _____

   _____

By now, you would have got a glimpse of your true identity. Various exercises that we did through the book so far, would have made you aware that your true identity is beyond what is seen. You are a conscious point of light, a living light that gives life to the body.

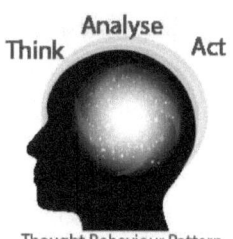

Thought Behaviour Pattern

You are the one who thinks, feels, makes judgments, and creates thought-behaviour patterns. You are the one who experiences feelings and emotions in various situations. The body is an external form that can be seen.

Awareness of Your True Identity

To understand awareness, let's take 'X' as something that you would like to be aware of.

Thinking is when your mind creates thoughts about 'X'. Awareness is when you consciously observe and your attention is focused on 'X'. Awareness is created when Thoughts and Feelings are directed towards 'X'.

In this chapter let us learn how to create awareness of the self – which is also called self-realisation by many philosophers and spiritualists.

Focusing your attention inward on yourself can be done through creating thoughts about who you are beyond the body. Connecting with radiant energy residing within the body and is thinking and feeling every moment.

Let us take some moment and have first-hand experience of the Being and its innate values or nature.

Experiential Exercise:

"Sit in a quest place undistracted from an external world. Examine where is your attention at the moment. Are you focused on reading these words and are deeply connected to these words? Are you unknowingly also aware of the surroundings? Do not let go of your attention to the inside world and become deeply rooted within.

Feel the inner beam of energy within – the one who is absorbed in the experience of these words. Observe how focusing inside changes your state of awareness. Are you able to experience the stillness of the body and the mind? Where did this stillness emerge? It emerged from within you. Know that you are peace – your true nature.. continue to be in that experience for a couple of more moments."

Reflection:

1. Describe your experience of the above exercise in the below space.

_____

_____

_____

_____

2. Were you able to experience the stillness within?

   ☐ Yes   ☐ No

Even during the day while you are doing everything at an external level, continue to feel the Being, the Energy within. This will enable you to live life more deeply and reach your inner spaces which you may have never explored.

It is easy to be connected with your inner stillness when you are connected within. Then external realities of life will not affect you as much because your sense of stability comes from within. Once you practice this inner-connectedness, even the most challenging situations will turn into an opportunity to go deep within. While continuing to do everything outside, there will be a deep sense of stability and calmness.

It is like a tree that is deeply rooted and grounded that no external winds can shake or break. The deeper the roots of the tree, the stronger it grows up to be.

Similarly, when we are internally rooted, we flourish at an external level, because our mind is stable, our decisions are balanced, and there is clarity in priorities. All this makes us flourish at an external level while being still and calm inside.

Remember how a mother, while doing all the work, manages to keep her one eye on the child. While she continues to do chores, she still keeps checking if the child needs anything.

It's exactly like that, while doing everything externally, keep an eye of attention on your inner environment – is your mind crying (sad thoughts), is your mind cranky (irritated thoughts)..? While doing everything externally, keep your inner environment your priority, like a child is to the mother.

The true nature of the Being

The first and foremost experience that you will have, when you go within and disconnect your mental cords from the external world is a deep sense of stillness and calmness. This is because you are connected to the Being – that is peaceful. This is the reason why you can't get angry all day or remain irritable all day. Even if you are mad at someone, you will come back to peace. It is like water – you boil water but it will come back to its normal temperature.

Peace is an innate value of the Being.

However, today we are seeking peace because the Being on this human journey has experienced anger, stress, irritation, etc. But is always wanting to go back to peace.

Similarly, innate values of the Being like love, happiness, power, wisdom, purity, and bliss are all residing within us. The only effort is to let go of the chattering of the mind and allow these innate values to emerge through the self.

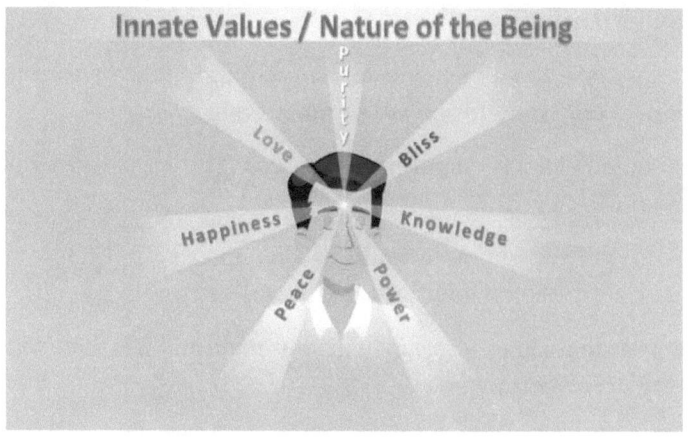

Initially, it may be a bit of an effort to go back to these innate values as you haven't deeply experienced them for long. In the past, you may only have had glimpses of experience of these values. You may have got temporary experience of love in relationships, but not an unconditional one. You may have had an experience of happiness from acquiring something, however, it is not a permanent experience of happiness.

This is because we are seeking intrinsic values of the Being from the externalities of the world. What we get from the external world is limited and temporary. Whereas the Being and its innate / core values are permanent in this temporary world.

So, you may ask, if it is within me, why can't I access and experience it at all points in time?

Let's say there is a file in your office storage that contains very important documents. However, it is not something that you use very often. Chances are when you need that file, you may take some time to find it. It may also happen that other files that you use very often (anger, irritation, etc) are easily available to you and you can find them easily.

Experiential Exercise:

Let us take some moments and go within to reach out to the core of our being to access our innate values.

Sit quietly for a few moments. Your body is still, and so is your mind.

Focus your attention on your breath – in and out. Follow the natural rhythm of your breath – in and out.

Repeat these lines to yourself in your mind and feel these lines very deeply within you.

I am a Peaceful Being. I can access my calmness and stillness within.

I am a Happy Being. Happiness is an inner thing. It is who I am. I experience it fully.

I am a Loving Being. The love within me enables me to give unconditional love to everyone. I accept and understand everyone around me.

I am a Powerful Being. I have the inner strength and courage to face every life situation. I experience power within me fully and completely.

I am a Pure Being. The pure innocence of a child is radiated through me. This is who I am.

I am a Wise Soul. True knowledge of myself and the world around me makes me full of wisdom.

I am full of Bliss. A Blissful Being, bliss that goes beyond pleasures of the senses. True bliss is beyond the senses. It is my true nature.

These values complete me. I radiate these values to the world. I am full of these innate values and can access them every time I choose to look within.

Awareness of the Being creates pure consciousness through which the innate values are experienced and expressed at a deeper level. In this state, you are more aware of life. This is far from the current human consciousness which is lost in thinking of the mind. Experiencing and expressing the innate values raised our energy field wherein no external form of negativity can have an influence. Unaffected and uninfluenced, you continue to remain in this pure consciousness which enables you to radiate the same to everyone you meet.

Experiential Exercise:

Do this exercise early in the morning when you wake up, while you are still resting on the bed, and before starting your day's chores.

Pick up one innate value each day. For example: Peace

Keep your eyes half open. Lie on the back straight.

Flood your consciousness with the energy of peace. Experience peace deeply within you. You are peace. experience this line, Repeat it to yourself a few times.

Then feel that each part of your body is receiving the vibrations of peace from your toe to your head (feet, knees, abdomen, lungs, shoulder, arms, hands, face, forehead…)

And then back again from your head to your toe.

Flood your entire body with peace. Every cell, every organ is filled with this life energy.

Slowly radiate this energy around you as if it is creating an energy field around you.

Stay with that feeling for a few moments before you are ready for the day.

Think-A-Thon

- ❖ You are a conscious point of light, a living light that gives life to the body.

- ❖ You are the one who thinks, feels, makes judgments, and creates. You are the one who experiences feelings and emotions.

- ❖ Innate values of the Being like peace love, happiness, power, wisdom, purity, and bliss are all residing within you.

- ❖ Awareness of the Being creates pure consciousness through which the innate values are experienced and expressed at a deeper level.

9. Awakening to a Conscious Way of Living

Exercise 1:

Part A: Read the below text in 15 Seconds.

Itisabasichumanemotionthateveryhumanbeingisseekingorlookingforveryhardandyetpeoplefinditdifficulttofindevenadaywherethereisconstantfeelingofhappinessthroughouttheday

Reflection

1. Was it easy or was it difficult to read the above text compared to the other text in this book?

   _____

2. Was it more time-consuming or less time-consuming to read the above text compared to the other text in this book?

   _____

3. Did you have to make assumptions about words written?

   _____

Part B: Read the below text in 15 Seconds.

> Happiness is a basic human emotion that every human being is seeking or looking for, very hard. And yet people find it difficult to find even a day where there is constant feeling of happiness throughout the day.

Reflection

1. Was it easy or was it difficult to read the above text compared to the other text in this book?

   _____

2. Was it more time-consuming or less time-consuming to read the above text compared to the other text in this book?

   _____

3. Did you have to make assumptions about words written?

   _____

4. What was the difference between the text in part A and part B of the exercise?

   _____
   _____

As you would have correctly pointed out, the difference between the text in part A and part B of the exercise is that part B had spaces, punctuation marks, and appropriate upper case and lower case in the text.

Just by adding spaces, punctuation marks, and appropriate upper case and lower case in the text, the text became easy to read, less time-consuming, and also you did not have to make assumptions about the words written because you could exactly read words.

This is exactly how our consciousness works. If we live an unaware life, lost in our mind with no full stop to unwanted thoughts, no spaces with a continuous stream of thoughts; we find life to be complicated and we keep making assumptions about life situations. This impacts all aspects of life – our relations, our decisions, and our overall experience of life.

Research suggests that for most of the human beings living today, more than 90% of their thoughts are:

1. either waste or repetitive - which means we do not put those thoughts into action
2. or negative – thoughts that make us feel uncomfortable or depleted

That is where conscious living plays a role in helping us come back to our peaceful selves. When we are living a conscious or aware life, we do not get lost in thoughts and are consciously able to choose the right kind of thoughts and feelings. Once we consciously choose the right thoughts over a period of time, they become our natural nature too. Then we need not make a conscious effort to think right but consciousness becomes our way of living. After all, anything that we practice becomes natural to us.

Why do we lose our Consciousness?

Exercise:

Write your introduction in 5 to 7 lines, the way you would introduce yourself to a stranger and you want them to know you.

_____
_____
_____
_____
_____
_____
_____
_____

Write your strengths and weaknesses in the below space.

_____
_____
_____
_____
_____
_____
_____

Ask yourself, are you really all that you mentioned above?

Is this who you are or are these labels you have acquired from external authorities?

We are born human beings, but as we go along we keep acquiring labels. The first label that we get when we are born, is that of a gender. Then the family, religion, nationality, education, professions, and so on. We also get labels based on certain patterns of behaviour we exhibit (I am too quiet, she is too sensitive and so many more labels). As we go on acquiring these labels and attach our sense of self to these labels, we go on losing our consciousness and become more aware of the labels than who we are.

Example:

I place the first circle here:

Then I place the next circle, a little bigger than the first one over it.

Then I place the next circle, a little bigger than the second one over it.

Then I place the next circle, a little bigger than the third one over it.

Now what is visible is the bigger circle and the first original circle is lost somewhere in the process. This is what exactly happens with our original consciousness. We go on acquiring new circles of labels on our consciousness and lose awareness of our original consciousness. The biggest circle of labels is the label with which we are too attached. For example, some people are too attached to their label of gender as male or female. Some people are too attached to their label of their nationality and consider others less good or inferior and many such labels.

Whatever you are too attached to, pulls you more into unconsciousness.

With all the labels, one after the other, the original consciousness of the being is only 1% or less because we hardly define ourselves or experience ourselves based on our true identity.

Meditative Exercise to Drop all Labels and be ourselves:

Sit in silence for a few moments. Spend some time with yourself. Away from everything outside.

Bring all the labels you use to define who you are on the screen of your mind.

- Name
- Gender
- Family Name
- Religion
- Nationality
- Education Qualification

- Profession
- Relationship / Role
- Your opinion about yourself
- Other's opinion about you.

Ask yourself, are you really this?

One by one, drop these labels and let them go (for example: I am not this name – this is what is given to me by my family)

As you go on dropping the labels one by one, experience a sense of lightness that is growing within you as if some heavy burden is being taken away from you.

Drop your labels of strengths and weaknesses, as they are also given to you by society as a measure of social standards of these attributes.

How does it feel to drop all the labels?

Now, what remains is who you are. A conscious point of energy, an invisible light residing in this body.

Just be there, still, with this feeling for a few moments before you move to the next topic of this book. Cherish the feeling a bit more deeply.

Think-A-Thon

Write 3 Key Learnings you had from this Chapter on Awakening to a Conscious Way of Living.

❖

❖

❖

10. The Higher Consciousness

Hypothetical Situation:

You get to know that the world is going to end tomorrow and so you only have a day to live.

Reflection:

1. If you have a day to live, what would you like to do in a day?

   _____
   _____
   _____
   _____

2. How would you like to live your next 24 hours?

   _____
   _____
   _____
   _____

3. What unfinished business of this lifetime would you like to complete in this little time that you have?

   _____
   _____
   _____
   _____

4. Would you like to forgive someone and let go of the burden you may be carrying on your mind for long? If yes, whom would you like to forgive?

_____
_____
_____
_____

5. Would you like to ask for forgiveness from someone? If yes, from whom?

_____
_____
_____
_____

6. Do you think you have lived your life to the fullest?

_____
_____
_____
_____

7. Given a chance to live your life again, is there anything you would like to live differently? If yes, which part of your life?

_____
_____
_____
_____

Well, good news – the world is not going to end tomorrow.

But ask yourself, do you want to wait for that one last day to live your life to the fullest???

One of my friends, who works in the healthcare sector, once happened to share with me that there are times when he has to share with the patients that based on their physical condition, they may not be able to live long. Some of the patients have a week, some have a month, and some have a few months in hand.

However, every time he informs his patients of this dreadful news, almost all the patients have this common feeling –

✓ I have not lived my life enough.

✓ I was so busy making a living that I forgot to live.

✓ I was thinking I would just start living my life now and t happened to me.

When these people are asked, what is it that they would like to do if they had very little time on their hands before they leave this body, some of the common answers are:

✓ I would like to spend time with my loved ones.

✓ I would like to be happy and live life to the fullest.

✓ I would like to ask someone for forgiveness.

✓ I would like to forgive someone and let go of the burden

How good it would be to live life fully, every day. Instead of looking back one day and saying "I wish" I would have..

Reflection:

1. If you continue to live your life the way you are living right now till your last day and you look back at your life, how would you feel?

   _____
   _____
   _____
   _____

2. Ask yourself, what alterations you can make today so then on the last day when you look back – you have a sense of fulfilment and contentment.

   _____
   _____
   _____
   _____

There are so many trivial things that we stress over in life – traffic, weather, other people's behaviour, etc. These are exactly those things that will have no meaning when you evaluate your life.

Everything that you are stressing today to acquire - a lot of money, a bigger house, a better car, luxury travel, and holidays will just end up being momentary pleasures and will never last long.

Most people today are busy accumulating much more than they would ever need in their lifetime. Imagine not even being able to carry even a single bag out of everything that you are accumulating. What you will carry with you in your next lifetime is the blessings you have accumulated, the love that you carry in your heart, calmness that you have filled yourself with.. but most of us are losing these to accumulate everything that is not even going to last one lifetime. Isn't this the irony of our lives today?

Living a life full of blessings, compassion, kindness, gratitude, and a helping hand to someone in need.. is all that will matter in the end to the self and to the Higher Power, the Supreme.

Connecting with Higher Power

In a world where peace, love, and happiness seem to be rare, the world where anger, hatred, and unhappiness have become an everyday experience, the role of the One – who is ever-giving and ever-loving comes into the picture.

When all the beings have drifted away from their core values of peace, love, and happiness, the bestower of happiness is called upon to help us re-emerge our innate values, the one who is always full of these values and never loses them. The one who is a constant benefactor to all human souls.

We may consider the Supreme as some distant entity but the truth is that the Supreme is like a loving parent who is always there to take care of us. Thoughts and Feelings are the way to be able to connect and receive blessings of the Supreme.

A realisation that the Supreme Being is just a thought away, is so comforting in times when we have distanced ourselves for many many births.

Just like water flows from a higher source to a lower source effortlessly. Similarly, the remembrance of the Supreme makes peace, love, power, and happiness flow from the Supreme Being to all human beings. It is in the form of blessings that the soul / being receives the energy or vibrations which cannot be seen through these eyes, but the eye of the mind, and can be experienced by the soul.

It is the experience all Human Souls are longing today for.

The Call of the Time

It is a time when many people are adapting to yoga, meditation, and spirituality in their lives. More than ever before, Spiritual revolution and evolution is taking place where not only old aged people but even youth and children feel the need to learn meditation and practice spirituality in one form or another.

This is exactly a sign that the world is going through some sort of transformation where more and more souls want to go back to their core nature and the innate values of the being.

Like a cycle of Day and Night, there is darkness in the minds of souls and so everyone is waiting for a bright day to emerge where the light of peace, love, power, and happiness is the most natural way of living. We are looking for it, consciously or unconsciously, because we know it does exist, it is not a fancy or a myth but a reality we have lived.

It is time to Enlighten ourselves with these values. Enlightenment here only means rising above all that we are not, ego, the false identity, and awakening to the pure being beyond the name and form. This is the journey and this is the destination too.

When you are on a journey, it is good to know where you are heading, so you know the directions in which you would like to move ahead. But at the same time, the only reality of the journey is every step that you are taking at the moment. The awareness that you create at this moment is all that is the reality.

The collection of these moments will together become your life. The effort here is as simple as this, being in an enlightened state in this moment, and then the next moment, and then the next moment. Moment by moment, when these moments are collected will sum up to be your life. And that is the way to live a whole and complete life – a life that is fully lived.

A being is whole and complete by itself, and doesn't need anything extra from outside to complete itself – neither relations nor possessions. The only effort is to uncover these layers one by one and let the original pure self emerge from the acquired layers.

The presence of the Supreme in your awareness and the remembrance of the Supreme makes it easier to allow your original self to emerge. The pure and elevated consciousness of the Supreme being brings out and emerges our own pure elevated consciousness. This makes our return journey towards our enlightened state smooth and effortless.

Ask yourself – are you ready for it?

Think-A-Thon

Write 3 Key Learnings you had from this Chapter on The Higher Consciousness

❖

❖

❖

11. Surrender – the Ultimate Human Experience

Reflection

1. Is there any life situation that you are finding unsatisfactory or intolerable?

    A. Describe the situation in a few words:

    _____
    _____
    _____

    B. Describe your feelings towards the situation in a few words:

    _____
    _____
    _____

2. How are you currently managing the situation?

    A. Internally (Thoughts and Emotions)

    _____
    _____
    _____

    B. Externally (Action / Behaviour)

    _____
    _____
    _____

Imagine you are driving on a highway at night and there is thick Fog along the way. You would immediately turn on the Fog light which is like a flashlight cutting through the Fog and creating a clear way in front of you.

Fog are the life situations that you term as unsatisfactory or intolerable. Surrender is a flashlight that cuts through the Fog and creates clear consciousness for you to get through the situation. Surrender breaks the unconscious resistance pattern.

Surrender means to say "Yes" to whatever life is offering in the present. Surrender is understanding that there is a higher purpose for everything that is happening. When you surrender, you work along with the universe and spiritual laws of higher purpose instead of working against it. It enables you to connect with your inner stillness, the deeper reality of being which allows you to bring peace and calmness to your thoughts, words, and actions

Surrender is a simple yet profound state of mind where you do not oppose life instead go with its flow.

Is surrender a sign of weakness?

Surrender is not giving up or a weak state of mind where you do not want to take action or do nothing about a situation. In reality, surrender is totally aligned with taking action and initiating change. It only brings about a shift in your way of being and experiencing life in any situation.

For example:

You are going from the ground floor to the 3rd floor and you get stuck in an Elevator or a lift. So, surrender doesn't mean you don't ring a bell or inform authorities by reaching out.

You do not give up and stay stuck in an elevator. Nor do you deny that there is a need for action, you do.

You just do not label the situation as unfair, negative, intolerable, etc. You shift your attention away from any form of judgment about the situation and once you accept the reality of the current moment you are far more capable of managing the situation by clear thinking and the right action to come out of that situation.

Non-surrender makes your inner state rigid and emerges ego in the form of more resistance. More ego means more suffering, more suffering means radiating negative energy to the universe and the situation you are resisting. This makes the situation even more intense. Whatever you give your energy to, it grows.

There is an old saying – wherever attention goes, energy flows. Wherever energy flows, that grows.

Resisting a situation only gives it more energy and thus such a situation, in one form or another, persists in our lives.

Any things that you accept fully will take you from non-peace to peace.

Surrender in Action

The way to break this pattern or cycle of repeated unwanted situations is by complete surrender.

Exercise to practice surrender:

Step 1: Acknowledging that there is resistance within you.

Step 2: Observe the labels (bad, unfair, etc.) that the mind is giving to the situation.

Step 3: Feel the Energy of the emotions you are experiencing while you label the situation.

Step 4: Slowly detach yourself from the labels of good or bad.

Step 5: Acknowledge the "is-ness" of every moment – tell yourself: 'It is what it is'.

Step 6: Say 'YES' to everything that is in this moment.

Step 7: Surrender to life and allow it to operate through you.

Step 8: Allow the higher purpose to take charge of your life and work along with it.

When you practice surrender, a spiritual dimension opens up within you where no external reality can make you vulnerable and weak. It makes you so much more stable and at peace within yourself and external situations lose their power over you.

Surrender to the Divine

The ultimate human experience is to be able to surrender to the Divine Power and know that nothing ever can go wrong when you are in the canopy of Blessings from the Divine power.

Surrender to the Divine is the highest spiritual attainment where you trust that you and your life are a prerogative of the Supreme Divine Being.

When you operate from this mindset, you see how your trials will turn into triumphs, your pain will turn into gains, and your story into glory. This is the magic of surrender to the Divine or the Supreme Being.

Think-A-Thon

- ❖ Surrender means to say "Yes" to whatever life is offering to you in the present.
- ❖ Surrender is a simple yet profound state of mind where you do not oppose life instead go with its flow.
- ❖ Any things that you accept fully will take you from non-peace to peace.

www.ingramcontent.com/pod-product-compliance
Lightning Source LLC
LaVergne TN
LVHW041613070526
838199LV00052B/3120